Wishing you well with roses,
For a rose means thoughts of love.
Wishing you well with sunbeams
That are blessings from above.

Wishing you well with snatches of a song
And silent prayer.
Spending a quiet moment
And wishing you were there.

In the shadow of old buildings
Time worn landmarks, rain washed stone
Thinking of you and wondering
Where all the time has flown.

In the glory of a landscape
Or the shelter of a tree
Wherever there is solace
And serenity.

Wishing you well with memories
For sweet thoughts bring you near.
Wishing you well with all our love
Because you are so dear.

Faversham is a charming old Kentish town which once served as a busy seaport. The visitor can still find much of interest here, such as the timbered Guildhall in the Market Place, and this colourful and ornate village pump.

LOOKING AHEAD

May you see beyond the grimy buildings
To all the glory of the highest hill.
May you look beyond the cares of living
To where the promised joy is shining still.

May you see between the narrow roadways
To all the clover growing in the green
Heeding not the turmoil of existence
Because a blackbird sings above the scene.

A fine view of Edinburgh can be had from the elevation of Calton Hill (*left*). Galashiels (*below*) manages to retain its beauty despite the constant pall of smoke which issues from its factories engaged in the manufacture of tweed.

LIFE IN THE OPEN AIR

The health of the moorland is yours for a tonic
The wealth of the wildflowers are strewn at your feet
The gold of the sunbeams are radiant blessings
The scent of the heather is wholesome and sweet

There is a freedom away from the cities
The wandering wayside steals peace from the earth.
Linger and listen to all the small murmurs
Of life in the soil and the stirring of birth.

The hopes of a lifetime gleam on the horizon
The past and the future are fused into one
The happiest moments encircle the present
And back on the track are the years that are gone.

Better to live than to think about living,
Better to feel than to fear what must be.
Better to love and be gracious in giving
To breathe and to listen, to touch and to see.

The world is a gift and the day is a keepsake
Happy the heart with the will to employ it
Take all the beauty, the light and the loving
Thank God for good health and the time to enjoy it.

Pony-trekking is the ideal mode of travel for those who wish peacefully yet thoroughly to explore the beauties of the English countryside. Here, the ponies wend their way across the heather-carpeted downs of Exmoor, in Somerset.

HAPPY DAYS

Flowers make the memories
Of all our happy days.
They blossom with our loveliest thoughts
Enrich our sunlit ways.

The rain upon a petal
Glistens as the tears of grief
Where the sunshine and the sentiment
Both beautify the leaf.

Climbing plants are a boon to any garden, and ideal for disguising unsightly walls. The clematis 'Nelly Moser' (*below*) is a firm favourite with flower lovers, and the dazzling blooms of *Camellia japonica* 'Jupiter' (*right*) add a hint of the exotic to the most ordinary garden.

HARMONY AND HOPE

While there's a timbered cottage
And a hamlet 'neath a hill
An inn sign swinging in the wind
A field to plough and till.

A crooked street, a lattice window
Hung with flowers in season
A peal of bells that still proclaims
The age, the time, the reason.

A scene of harmony and hope
Where age and beauty blend.
A place to take refreshment
And to meet a loyal friend.

A cosy room, a shelf of books
To make a leisured choice
While waiting for a simple meal
And well-beloved voice.

While there's a spire against the sky
And cattle idly grazing,
There will be peace within the heart
That finds the time for lazing.

Ledbury, in Herefordshire, is one of England's many rural beauty spots, far removed from modern architecture. The quaint upper storeys of Elizabethan houses overhang narrow Church Lane, and the scene is dominated by the lofty spire of the sixteenth-century church.

'Even the weariest river winds somewhere safe to sea'

ON THE TIDE OF LIFE

In the ripple of a river
In a house beneath a hill
May you find the hidden secret
That is life, come good, come ill.

With humour in the common round
And joy in simple pleasures
Wherever life may lead you
May you gather countless treasures.

This fine view across Loch Long (*left*) shows the grassy slopes of Ben Lomond in the distance. England is well known for its delightful country cottages – Weston Court (*below*) is one of Warwickshire's many lovely thatched buildings.

'When doth thy sweet and quiet eye look through its fringes
to the sky'

JOY OF LIVING

Above the lapping ocean
Where the gulls are flying high
Is the freedom of the firmament
And wisdom of the sky.

In the bosom of the billows
That have rocked the stars to rest
The purpose of existence
Overall is manifest.

For what is more important
When a gull is flying free
Than the majesty of life
Above the vast expanse of sea?

Ambition simply satisfied
To glory and to give
In exhilerating movement
Just to breathe, to eat, to live.

The high ambitions of mankind
For grandeur, gold and greed
Against the beauty of the scene
Look very small indeed.

The brilliant blue of the sky in Scotland is here almost indistinguishable from the sea. This is the route of the Mallaig to Skye Ferry, and the mewing seagulls habitually follow in its wake, hoping for scraps of food.

THROUGH LIFE'S LATTICE

May life repay the joy that you have given
And offer you a smile for every tear.
A smoother road to every hill you travel
A happy end to every busy year.

May all your troubles have a sunny window
To look ahead upon a brighter view
A heart that soars above the petty problems
To see the distant day that breaks anew.

Westminster Abbey in all its Gothic majesty (*left*) is one of London's most impressive sights. Castle Campbell, Clackmannanshire (*below*), is also Gothic and was originally called the Castle of Gloom, probably because it is perched in solitary splendour on a steep hill surrounded by rocky gorges.

Sing a song of sailing
Past the rivers and the streams
In the waters of contentment
To the harbour of your dreams.

With hope an ever guiding star
And faith to shine before
Leaving all the carking cares
Upon the rocky shore.

England's Island Heritage ensures that boating will never lose
its popularity here, whether one prefers the yachts at Pwllheli
Harbour in Caernarvonshire (*left*), or the beautifully decorated
traditional barge seen (*below*) plying the Llangollen Canal.

GOLDEN PROMISES

The pulse of Spring is throbbing
And the daffodils are bobbing
Waiving gallant trumpets to the sun.
To let the world be knowing
The merriment of growing
As they dance until their little day is done.

What faith to break the frozen sod
With golden promises from God
Showing that the Spring will never fail!
Bringing courage to the world
With every cheerful cup uncurled
That happiness and humour may prevail.

We, too, must struggle from the gloom
To lift our lives and let them bloom
In such a way that golden kindness spills.
Shaking off the rain of tears
And all the troubles of the years
To be as sunny as the daffodils.

Hyde Park Corner in spring adds a welcome splash of colour
to the huge metropolis of London. Amid this riot of daffodils,
the tired visitor can forget the jostling crowds and traffic, and
imagine himself in the heart of the country.

THE BIG DECISION

Over the hurdle, the test well done
The fear is over, the battle won.
You didn't fail and you didn't fall
It wasn't a bad jump after all.

One problem cleared, you can laugh at fate
Over the top and on the straight
A big decision, a night of pain
And nothing can be so bad again.

Show-jumping is a typically English sport, drawing vast crowds with its colour and excitement. Here (*left*), a horse clears the jump with consummate grace and ease, and the proud winners line up their horses to receive their rewards (*below*).

'To its own impulse every creature stirs'

MAGNIFICAT

Her coat is sheer perfection
Marked in subtle symmetry
The way she sits and grooms herself
Is beautiful to see.

Dainty as a lady
And a high born one at that
With grace in every movement
A delightful little cat.

But it is the lovely eyes of her
That seem to reach your heart,
To get her fancies gratified
Is such a simple art.

Magnificent she is
With not a whisker out of place
And such a saintly look
Upon her wistful little face.

Everybody knows her
For she is the Vicar's cat
And when they named her that is why
They chose "MAGNIFICAT".

The wistful yet knowing expression of this tabby cat makes it easy to understand why earlier civilisations treated these animals with such reverence. All cats, regardless of pedigree, possess a dignity of bearing and a love of independence which no mere human can quell.

SERVICE AND SONG

To the songs that are not written
To the poems in the heart
To the life that is a story
Told with courage from the start.

To the valour unrecorded
And the sacrifice unknown
God sees and weighs it all
And His reward in time is shown.

The attractive fishing village of Mevagissey in Cornwall (*left*) has a fine harbour for those who enjoy 'messing about in boats'. Newhaven (*below*) is a small port in Sussex – the picture shows a local fisherman intent on mending his nets.

'O'er the rose a veil of moss the angel throws'

ROSES FOR REMEMBRANCE

The roses whisper sweet secrets
Of friendship, fancy and fun
And the air is laden with perfume
When the life of the rose is done.

There are folds for a shadow to nestle
As they might in a silken sheet
And dewdrops sparkle and glisten
Where the taste of the nectar is sweet.

There are dimples and smiles that shimmer
For a delicate breeze that blows
And a prayer that lurks in a petal
With a blessing of sweet repose.

It's a token of love for the lover
And a gift for the ailing soul
A prize for the special grower
And a constant joy in a bowl.

The sweetest scent in the garden
Of the loveliest flower that grows
Is born to bring comfort to someone
With hope from the heart of the rose.

The rose is the emblem of England and the best loved of all our flowers, gracing many an English garden. This regal bloom with its delicate, almost translucent pink petals and lush green foliage, is aptly named 'Royal Highness'.

CITY OF LAUGHTER AND TEARS

Give a smile and share a sorrow
Meet a stranger, help a friend.
Cheer a neighbour, love a baby
Find a breaking heart to mend.

Every city asks for kindness
In the gaiety and glow
Underneath the noise and bustle
There is grief that does not show.

There are fears that are not noticed
In a fashionable dress
And the sparkle of a gem
That has the look of happiness.

We walk the pavements of the world
When jostling with a city crowd
So lift the cares of others near you
Even though your heart is bowed.

Courtesy will plant a sunbeam
For somebody in the day.
A passing kindness or a smile
Will send a worry on its way.

Piccadilly Circus seems like the hub round which London revolves. Those who gather round the statue of Eros will always find something of interest to watch, especially at night when the gaudy advertisements are transformed into a dazzling neon display.

THE BEST FRIEND

Give to me the character
Warm hearted, kind and gay
His accent doesn't matter
If he has true words to say.

A cheerful manner is the equal
Of a clever mind.
An open heart is just as precious
As a purse gold lined.

Pulls Ferry (*below*) is a picturesque old water-gate behind Norwich Cathedral – the stones used to build the cathedral were brought here by barge. The Glenfinnan Memorial, Inverness (*right*), commemorates the spot where Prince Charles Stewart unfurled his banner in 1745.

'Be suffering what it may Time will bring summer'

GOOD WISHES FOR YOUR WELFARE

In distance you are miles away
Yet very close you seem today
With everything we say and do
We cannot help but think of you.

With every song, with every joke
It is the same as if you spoke
We all hope that your health is mending
Because our wishes are unending.

This plain granite church in Crathie, Royal Deeside (*left*), is attended by the Royal Family when they stay at nearby Balmoral. The fantastic Culzean Castle (*below*) stands on a huge rock, at whose foot are the Caves of Culzean, reputedly haunted by fairies.

HAVEN OF DREAMS

Perhaps when you are thinking
Of a good friend whom you miss
Of a time of great rejoicing
Or an hour of perfect bliss.

Maybe your name is mentioned
As their name slips from your tongue
And in your different spheres
You bless the days when you were young.

In the splendour of a coastline
Or the glory of a view
No doubt that very character
In thought is close to you.

For the link of love is lasting
When the feeling is profound
And the years between are nothing
In a great world turning round.

Perhaps when you are dreaming
And the light of memory beams
All the happy times are mirrored
In the river of your dreams.

Fraserburgh, Aberdeenshire, is a lovely little town with quaint old houses sloping down to its water's edge where the colourful fishing boats are moored. Its fine harbour has brought prosperity to the town as it is an excellent centre for herring fishing.

NESTING TIME

A bird's wing is a lovely thing
With feathers overlapping.
A bird's nest, where an egg may rest
Snug in its leafy wrapping.

Is such a secret sight to see
The wonder has no words
God surely cares for us
Who cares so well for beasts and birds.

Birds employ a natural cunning to avoid their enemies. The
coot (*left*) weaves an intricate nest of reeds, well hidden from
the eyes of predators, while the woodcock (*below*) boasts an
amazingly effective camouflage as it scuttles back to its nest.

HEART'S DESIRE

Green leaves and dappled shadows
And a pathway through the trees
Overhanging branches
Making music with the breeze.

A sweet September morning
When the mist has rolled away
And left a sparkling splendour
Full of fragrance for the day.

Just to be alive
Is almost more than we deserve
To share this day, this gift of God's
To breathe, to work, to serve.

Lovely in entirety
Goodwill, good health, good friends
In the beauty of existence
On which life itself depends.

What more could any heart request
In vistas far and wide
Than a meadow in the sunshine
And a gentle horse to ride.

Every little girl has dreamed of owning a pony, and for these three, the wish has come true. Ponies need a lot of care and attention, but a brisk canter through the woods makes all the hard work seem worthwhile.

'The night is mother of the day'

THINKING OF YOU

I shall be wishing you well, my dear
Whenever my thoughts fly free.
When the shadows lengthen and day grows tired
And the sun sets over the sea.

And I shall be wishing you well, my dear
Hoping and praying still
When the moon and the stars have veiled their light
And the dawn climbs over the hill.

Scotland has always been associated with romance and the supernatural. Here (*below*), the setting sun bathes the Nith Estuary in a mysterious golden haze, while the ruins of Kilchurn Castle add an eerie quality to the waters of Loch Awe (*right*).

'A dewy freshness fills the silent air'

MORNING GLORY

When dawn breaks on a frosty morning
We think of you and yours
And as the chorus of the birds
Grows louder out of doors.

The memories come faster,
All the foolishness and fun
Comes flowing back to meet us
With the first burst of the sun.

When the world is white with wonder
And the air is fresh and free
And the breezes are so buoyant
That they shed the tang of sea.

Then there seems to be a moment
When the world is in accord
And the mountains pass the message
To be still and praise the Lord.

And that's the time to take fresh heart
In all life's stony ways
In sorrow or in sickness
Hope renewed brings brighter days.

One of the most beautiful sights in the Lake District are the
twin peaks of the Langdale Pikes, their snowy coat glistening
against the deep blue of the sky. Huddling beneath these
towering heights is the rugged and remote Langdale Valley.

'I have not made the world. He that made it will guide me'

THE OPEN DOOR

Every big decision is the gateway
"Do" or "Dare".
The future is unknown
But opportunity is there.

Fate unlocks the door
For the retreat or the advance
May God bless your decisions
When you dare to take a chance!

Cambridge offers a wealth of romantic architecture amongst her many famous colleges. The Bridge of Sighs which crosses the Cam (*below*), evokes all the charm of Venice, and the Caius Gate of Honour (*right*) is a superb Renaissance gateway leading to Caius College.

THE HAND OF A FRIEND

How big the world,
How many people crowd into a city
A friend for every friend
And that is why it seems a pity.

That there are lonely people
Even in a crowded place
Who long to hear a cheery word,
Or see a smiling face.

Who have to go and jostle with the masses
To rejoice
That the warm heart of humanity
Is in a stranger's voice.

Among the crowd is somebody
With name as yet unknown
Who also walks nearby
And is attuned to them alone.

May fate be kind this day
With all this mass of hearts for blending
And bring a friend to meet a lonely heart
That needs befriending.

The hustle and bustle of Petticoat Lane, London's most famous stall market, creates a kaleidoscope of gay colour and noise. The market only opens on Sunday and is always crowded as it is a favourite hunting-ground for young and old alike.

'As long as life endures I feel I shall owe you a debt'

A FRIEND IN NEED

You were our friend when kindly words were needed
You helped us out when trouble came along.
It was through you our enterprise succeeded,
Through you we passed from sorrow into song.

What can we do to offer compensation?
What can we say explaining how we feel?
How can we show our great appreciation
For friends that are so ready and so real?

All the best riders start young, even if they do need a little
help from their friends (*left*). Horses naturally need a lot of
exercise, and the early morning is the most refreshing time
for a brisk trot or an amble through the fields (*below*).

'Love thou thy land with love far brought out of the storied past'

STORIES IN STONES

Beautiful Edinburgh
Queen of the North
Where scholars and princes
And courage come forth.

Cradle of History,
Home of the Bruce
Where the poorest or proudest
Success may produce.

Bastions and battlements
Cobbles and trees
Parks for the pleasure
Of sitting at ease.

Castle and College,
Candle and book
History lies
In each cranny and nook.

City of triumph
Of beauty untold
Where each stone underfoot
Is a story unrolled.

Edinburgh is a fascinating city, steeped in history and dominated by a rocky precipice with the castle on its summit. A magnificent panorama opens out from the viewing-platform on the castle's battlements, stretching over the New Town and down to the River Forth.

PUPPY FOR SALE

Whose hand will he be nuzzling
And whose voice will he obey?
Who will brush his coat
And take him walking every day?

He has to find a home
And from his mother must depart
Who will earn the love
That's in his loyal little heart?

The dog is Man's best friend – loyal, affectionate and a delightful companion. Few could resist the appealing eyes of this young Cocker Spaniel (*left*), while the two mischievous Alsatian pups (*below*) are longing for a boisterous game.

'Enough if at the end of all a little garden blossoms'

BLESS YOU

I bless your name in the morning
When the light is breaking through
Which seems a perfect time
To say a little prayer for you.

Then in the busy working hours
When break-time comes along.
The thoughts of you are singing
Like the chorus to a song.

And in the tranquil moments
The same old dream pursuing
Of "How you are?" and "Where you are?"
And what your hands are doing?

There really isn't any time
In any special day
When the wishes for your welfare
Are very far away.

At last when day is ending
And the evening shadows fall
A little blessing comes to mind
To wish you well, that's all.

The *Helleborous niger* is a beautiful flower more commonly known as the Christmas Rose. Despite its delicate appearance, it is a sturdy plant which thrives in rocky places and even survives a hard winter to decorate our tables at Christmas.

Every courteous action makes the world a better place,
No kindness is too limited to serve the human race.
No cheerful word is wasted and no sacrifice is lost
Sympathy and comfort are worth the time and cost.

In the homeliest circle can be found the power of peace
Blessings are far reaching, good relationships increase
The harmony of living that all friendly people spend
Builds a nobler world where goodwill rises in the end.

Many of Scotland's stately castles are now ruined, though Elcho Castle (*below*) is remarkably well preserved. The rugged, snow-tipped mountain of Ben Cruachan (3,689 feet) rears its head above the wooded shores and smooth waters of Loch Awe (*right*).

'Go shake the heather bells and make them ring each rosy bell'

LITTLE MIRACLES

He asked a miracle from Heaven
Some sign to prove Almighty God
And as he glanced towards the sky
His foot upon the heather trod.

He thought "There seems to be no proof
Of the Creator's Presence now"
But as he passed a rosy apple
Tumbled from a laden bough.

Still he walked and still be wondered
Looking for the Heavenly pledge
But failed to see the scarlet berries
Shining from the hoary hedge.

Not only in the clash of thunder
Or the Cross displayed above
Is the symbol of God's Kingdom
Or the glory of His Love.

Little miracles take place
Each day upon the earth
As much in human lives
As in the seasons' glowing birth.

Dolwyddelan Castle, steeped in tradition, stands a lonely guard over the wild Welsh valley of Caernarvonshire. Dating from 1170, it is now mostly in ruins, but the sturdy, square Norman keep still remains proudly erect.

AGE OF BEAUTY

Old churches that are touched with time's soft fingers
And moss-grown paths where memory still lingers.
Old arches where the stained glass windows dream
And cast reflections on the lazy stream.

Old coins, old brasses, pottery and plate
Ageless in beauty, never out of date.
Old haunts, like friendship that is born to last
Grow more precious as the years go past.

Ecclesiastical buildings were the most important form of architecture in bygone centuries. Wells Cathedral, Somerset (*left*), possesses the finest exterior of all British cathedrals, and Castle Acre Priory, founded in Norfolk in 1090, is still extremely beautiful despite its poor condition (*below*).

'Love is the beginning, the middle and the end of everything'

WELCOME HOME

Sunshine and the seasons
Play so great a part in life
A home without a cheerful heart
Is much inclined to strife.

And if a lovely character
Falls ill for just a while
The whole face of the earth
Awaits for the returning smile.

Norwich Cathedral, here viewed from the snow-carpeted Upper Close, is a majestic Norman structure founded in 1096.

Published and printed in Great Britain by Jarrold & Sons Ltd, Norwich
85306 450 4 © Jarrold & Sons Ltd, Norwich 174